P9-AOV-465

JAMESTOWN

Heritage

READERS

Pocketful
of Posies

Lee Mountain, Ed.D.
University of Houston, Texas

Sharon Crawley, Ed.D.
Florida Atlantic University

Edward Fry, Ph.D.
Professor Emeritus
Rutgers University

Jamestown Publishers
Providence, Rhode Island

Favorite Children's Classics

ILLUSTRATED BY THE BEST ARTISTS
FROM THE PAST AND PRESENT

Jamestown Heritage Readers, Pocketful of Posies
Catalog No. 949

© 1994 by Jamestown Publishers, Inc.

All rights reserved. The contents of this book are
protected by the United States Copyright Law. Address
all inquiries to Editor, Jamestown Publishers, Post
Office Box 9168, Providence, Rhode Island 02940.

Cover and text design by Patricia Volpe, based on an
original design by Deborah Hulsey Christie
Cover and border illustrations by Pamela R. Levy

Printed in the United States of America

1   2   3   4   5   HA   98   97   96   95   94

ISBN 0-89061-949-2

C·O·N·T·E·N·T·S

ONE
Rhymes Retold

TWO
Around Again

THREE

Animals from Here and There

FOUR

Say and Play

UNIT ONE
Rhymes Retold

Ring around a Rosie

Ring around a rosie,
A pocket full of posie.
Hush! Hush!
We all fall down.

Roses Are Red

Roses are red.
Violets are blue.
Sugar is sweet.
And so are you.

Here We Go Round
the Mulberry Bush

Here we go round the mulberry bush,
The mulberry bush, the mulberry bush.
Here we go round the mulberry bush,
So early in the morning.

This is the way we wash our hands,
Wash our hands, wash our hands.
This is the way we wash our hands,
So early in the morning.

This is the way we go to school,
Go to school, go to school.
This is the way we go to school,
So early in the morning.

12

HERE WE GO ROUND THE MULBERRY BUSH

13

UNIT TWO

Around
Again

The Girl Who Wished

Once there was a girl who worked in the garden of the Empress.

Each day she would pick flowers.

Then she would take them to a lady with a vase.

The lady would fix them in the vase for the Empress.

The girl was happy
working in the garden.

But one day she said,
"I would like to have a vase.
I would like to fix flowers
in a vase for the Empress."

The girl had been happy.
But now she was not happy.
She said, "I wish I were a lady
with a vase."

Her wish was heard.
Lightning flashed!
Thunder boomed.
She was a lady with a vase!

For a while, she was happy.
Each day she fixed flowers in a vase.
Then she took them to the Empress.

But one day she said,
"I would like to be the Empress."

She had been happy.
But now she was not happy.
She said, "I wish I were
the Empress."

Her wish was heard.
Lightning flashed!
Thunder boomed.
She was the Empress!

For a while, she was happy.
Each day her ladies fixed
vases of flowers for her.

But one day she said,
"I would like to pick
the flowers myself."

She had been happy.
But now she was not happy.
She said, "I wish I were the girl
who picked the flowers."

Her wish was heard.
Lightning flashed!
Thunder boomed.
She was herself again!

This time she stayed happy.
And never again did she wish
to be anyone but herself.

Wishes

Wishes, wishes
Won't wash dishes.

Mary, Mary, Quite Contrary

Mary, Mary, quite contrary,
How does your garden grow?
With silver bells and cockle shells,
And pretty maids all in a row.

27

The Little Old Woman
and Her Pig

A little old woman
found a sixpence.
She went to the market
and bought a pig.

On the way home
she came to a stile.

She wanted the pig
to jump over the stile.
But the pig would not do it.

The little old woman
saw a dog.

She said, "Dog!
Dog, bite pig.
Piggy won't get over the stile.
And I shan't get home tonight."

But the dog would not help.
The little old woman
saw a stick.

She said, "Stick!
Stick, beat dog.
Dog won't bite pig.
Piggy won't get over the stile.
And I shan't get home tonight."

31

But the stick would not help.
The little old woman
saw a fire.

She said, "Fire!
Fire, burn stick.
Stick won't beat dog.
Dog won't bite pig.
Piggy won't get over the stile.
And I shan't get home tonight."

But the fire would not help.
The little old woman
saw some water.

She said, "Water!
Water, quench fire.
Fire won't burn stick.
Stick won't beat dog.
Dog won't bite pig.
Piggy won't get over the stile.
And I shan't get home tonight."

But the water would not help.
The little old woman
saw an ox.

She said, "Ox!
Ox, drink water.
Water won't quench fire.
Fire won't burn stick.
Stick won't beat dog.
Dog won't bite pig.
Piggy won't get over the stile.
And I shan't get home tonight."

The ox said, "Bring me some hay.
Then I will drink the water."

So the woman brought the ox
some hay.

Then the ox began to drink the water.
The water began to quench the fire.

The fire began to burn the stick.
The stick began to beat the dog.

The dog began to bite the pig.
The pig jumped over the stile.

So the little old woman
did get home that night.

UNIT THREE

Animals from
Here and There

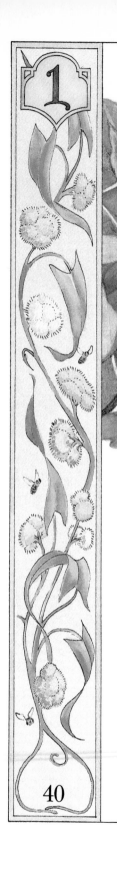

Anansi and the Leopard

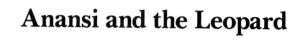

One day Anansi saw
the leopard sitting by a tree.

"Good day, my friend,"
said Anansi. "Will you play
a game with me?"

"I like to play games,"
said the leopard. "I like
to play almost as much
as I like to eat."

"I will tell you how we start
the game," said Anansi.
"First I will tie you up.
Then you will tie me up."

"Good," said the leopard.
He thought to himself,
"I will tie up Anansi.
Then I will eat him up."

While he was thinking,
he let Anansi tie him
to a tree.

42

43

Then Anansi said,
"I am like you, my friend.
I like to play almost as much
as I like to eat."

Anansi smiled. "Most of all
I like to play tricks on animals
who want to eat me up."

44

"I must go, my hungry friend,"
said Anansi with a laugh.
"I must go before you chew
through the ropes."

Anansi waved good-bye
to the leopard and ran away.

45

The Lion and the Unicorn

The lion and the unicorn
   Were fighting for the crown.

The lion beat the unicorn
   All around the town.

47

Some gave them white bread,
  And some gave them brown.

Some gave them plum cake
  And drummed them out of town.

49

The Bees and the Bear

The bees did not like the bear.
He was always taking their honey.
One day he saw a big beehive.

"Buzz," said the first bee.
"Do not take our honey."

"Grrr," said the bear.
"The honey is mine, mine, mine,
because I want it."

"No," said the first bee.
"It is ours because we make it.
Go away. I warn you."

But the bear did not go away.

"Buzz," said the second bee.

"Do not take our honey."

"Grrr," said the bear.

"The honey is mine, mine, mine,

because I want it."

"No," said the second bee.

"It is ours because we make it.

Go away. I warn you."

The bear still did not go away.
"Buzz," said the third bee.
"Do not take our honey."

"Grrr," said the bear.
"The honey is MINE, MINE, MINE,
because I want it."

"No," said the third bee.
"It is ours because we make it.
You have pushed too far."

All the bees buzzed out
from the hive.

They buzzed
around the bear's head.
They buzzed around his tail.
They chased him away
from the hive.

55

And what did the bear get
for all his "MINE, MINE, MINE"?
Many stings and no honey!

Take warning:
do not push too far.

A Bear Went over the Mountain

A bear went over the mountain,
A bear went over the mountain,
A bear went over the mountain,
To see what he could see.

The other side of the mountain,
The other side of the mountain,
The other side of the mountain,
Was all that he could see.

Sheep and Coyote

Coyote looked at Big Sheep
and Little Sheep. They knew
Coyote was hungry.

"Don't eat me," said Big Sheep.
"I would make you too full."

"Don't eat me," said Little Sheep.
"You would still be hungry."

"Maybe I will eat both of you,"
said Coyote.

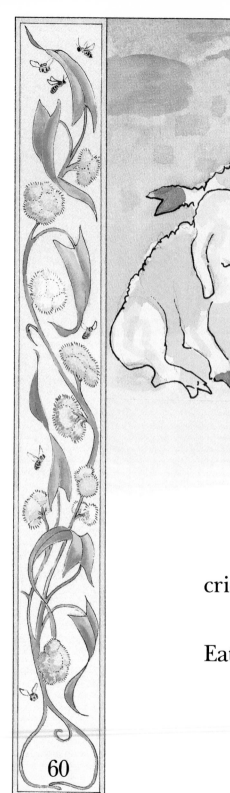

"Eat Little Sheep first!"
cried Big Sheep.

Little Sheep cried, "No!
Eat Big Sheep first."

Coyote thought, "I will have
some fun with these sheep.
Then I will eat both of them."

He drew a line across the road.
"You will race with each other,"
he said. "Then I will see
which one I will eat first."

Coyote turned to Big Sheep
and pointed **down** the road.
"You will start there," he said.

Then he turned to Little Sheep.
Coyote pointed **up** the road.
"You will start there," he said.

63

The sheep did as Coyote said.
They knew he could catch them
if they tried to run away.

Soon they were far apart.
Then Coyote said, "The first one
who gets back here wins. GO!"

Both sheep started running.
Coyote thought they would run
into each other.

But as the sheep ran,
they headed right at Coyote.

BOOM!

Down went Coyote!

The sheep kept on running.
By the time Coyote stood up,
the sheep were far away.
And they were laughing
at Coyote.

UNIT FOUR

Say and Play

Itsy Bitsy Spider

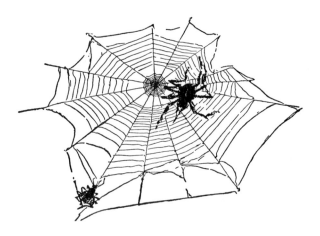

The itsy bitsy spider
Climbed up the water spout.
Down came the rain
And washed the spider out.

Out came the sun
And dried up all the rain.
And the itsy bitsy spider
Climbed up the spout again.

69

There Were Two Blackbirds

There were two blackbirds
Sitting on a hill,
The one named Jack,
The other named Jill.

Fly away, Jack!
Fly away, Jill!
Come again, Jack!
Come again, Jill!

The Farmer in the Dell

The farmer in the dell.
The farmer in the dell.
Hi-ho, the derry-o,
The farmer in the dell.

The farmer takes a wife.
The farmer takes a wife.
Hi-ho, the derry-o,
The farmer takes a wife.

The wife takes a child.
The wife takes a child.
Hi-ho, the derry-o,
The wife takes a child.

The child takes a nurse.
The child takes a nurse.
Hi-ho, the derry-o,
The child takes a nurse.

The nurse takes a dog.
The nurse takes a dog.
Hi-ho, the derry-o,
The nurse takes a dog.

The dog takes a cat.
The dog takes a cat.
Hi-ho, the derry-o,
The dog takes a cat.

The cat takes a rat.
The cat takes a rat.
Hi-ho, the derry-o,
The cat takes a rat.

The rat takes the cheese.
The rat takes the cheese.
Hi-ho, the derry-o,
The rat takes the cheese.

The cheese stands alone.
The cheese stands alone.
Hi-ho, the derry-o,
The cheese stands alone.

Diddle, Diddle, Dumpling

Diddle, diddle, dumpling,
My son John,
Went to bed
With his trousers on.

One shoe off,
One shoe on.
Diddle, diddle, dumpling,
My son John.

I·L·L·U·S·T·R·A·T·I·O·N C·R·E·D·I·T·S

Acknowledgment is gratefully made to the following for permission to reprint these illustrations.

PAGE	ILLUSTRATOR
8	Arthur Rackham. Courtesy of Blue Lantern Studio, Seattle, Washington.
9	L. Leslie Brooke.
10	Berta and Elmer Hader. From *Picture Book of Mother Goose* by Berta and Elmer Hader. © 1930, 1944, © renewed 1958, 1972 by Berta and Elmer Hader. Reprinted by permission of Outlet Book Company, a division of Crown Publishers, Inc.
11	Henriette Willebeek le Mair. © 1994 by Soefi Stichting Inayat Fundatie Sirdar. Reprinted by permission of East-West Publications (U.K.) Ltd.
12	Arthur Rackham. From *Mother Goose the Old Nursery Rhymes,* courtesy of the Providence Public Library, Edith Wetmore Collection of Children's Books.
13	Walter Crane. Courtesy of Blue Lantern Studio, Seattle, Washington.
16–24	Demi. © 1994 by Demi.
25	Tom Feelings. Used by permission of Tom Feelings. © by Tom Feelings.
26	Fanny V. Cory. Reprinted with permission of Macmillan Publishing Company from *The Fanny Cory Mother Goose.* © 1913, 1917 and renewed 1941, 1945 by Macmillan Publishing Company. Courtesy of Blue Lantern Studio, Seattle, Washington.

27   Dorothy Wheeler.

28–37   Frederick Richardson. From *Mother Goose Story Book,* Harris Collection of American Poetry and Plays, Brown University Library.

40–45   Jan Naimo Jones. © 1994 by Jamestown Publishers, Inc. All rights reserved.

46–49   L. Leslie Brooke. Reprinted from *Ring O' Roses,* published by The Albion Press Limited.

50   Charles Santore. From *Aesop's Fables* published by JellyBean Press, a division of dilithium Press, Ltd. © 1988 by Charles Santore. Used by permission of Charles Santore.

51–55   Pamela R. Levy. © 1994 by Jamestown Publishers, Inc. All rights reserved.

56   Milo Winter. From *The Aesop for Children* illustrated by Milo Winter. © 1919 by Checkerboard Press, Inc. Used with permission.

57   Pamela R. Levy. © 1994 by Jamestown Publishers, Inc. All rights reserved.

58–66   Shonto Begay. © 1994 by Jamestown Publishers, Inc. All rights reserved.

68   Jerry Pinkney. Reprinted by permission of the artist and Disney Press. © 1991 by Jerry Pinkney.

69   Jessie Willcox Smith.

70   Dorothy Wheeler.

71   Frederick Richardson. From *Mother Goose,* Harris Collection of American Poetry and Plays, Brown University Library.

72–77   Pamela R. Levy. © 1994 by Jamestown Publishers, Inc. All rights reserved.

78   Anne Anderson. From *The Old Mother Goose,* courtesy of the Providence Public Library, Edith Wetmore Collection of Children's Books.